CH0067l054

Herbal Teas, Tisanes, Plant-Based Teas & Tea Drinks

JESSIE OLESON MOORE
ILLUSTRATED BY JESSIE FORD

PHILADELPHIA

RP Minis®
Hachette Book Group
1290 Avenue of the Americas, New York, NY 10104
www.runningpress.com
@Running_Press

Printed in China

First Edition: March 2024

Published by RP Minis, an imprint of Hachette Book Group, Inc. The RP Minis name and logo is a registered trademark of Hachette Book Group, Inc.

Running Press books may be purchased in bulk for business, educational, or promotional use. For more information, please contact your local bookseller or the Hachette Book Group Special Markets Department at Special.Markets@hbgusa.com.

The publisher is not responsible for websites (or their content) that are not owned by the publisher.

Design by Amanda Richmond

Library of Congress Control Number: 2023939504

ISBN: 978-0-7624-8515-4

HH

10 9 8 7 6 5 4 3 2 1

CONTENTS

TEA DRINKS ... 91

Great love affairs
start with Champagne
and end with tisane.

—HONORÉ DE BALZAC

Herbal Teas, Tisanes, and Plant-Based Teas

───── ✦ ─────

Technically, herbal teas, or tisanes, are not "true" teas, meaning they are not made with the leaves of the

Camellia sinensis plant. Rather, they are made by infusing flowers, leaves, or really just about any plant-based ingredient (even non-herb ingredients, such as dried fruit) with hot water.

So why call them tea? A few reasons. First, while the key ingredient may be different, the process of steeping plant matter, then drinking it, is

pretty similar. Plus, we often drink herbal teas in the same spirit as tea—for relaxation, for health benefits, and as a social lubricant. Here are just a few of the countless "non-tea" infusions out there, ranging from the everyday to the exotic.

Amacha Tea: No sugar is necessary for this sweet-as-can-be Japanese tea. *Amacha* means "sweet tea" in Japanese and it delivers on that promise. It's made from the dried leaves of the *Hydrangea macrophylla*, which contains a compound called phyllodulcin, an all-natural sweetener that can be up to eight hundred times sweeter than sugar. This tea is often served on Buddha's birthday.

Arrowroot Tea: Arrowroot tea is a somewhat bitter tea made from the root of the kudzu plant (aka "Japanese arrowroot"), a tropical tuber. In Japan, arrowroot tea is traditionally sweetened and served as a sort of thick gruel-like mixture that's part dessert, part cure-all. In other parts of the world, Arrowroot tea is more likely to be made with dried arrowroot slices.

Barley Tea: Made by steeping roasted barley, this tea has a rich brown hue and a distinctive nutty flavor with a slightly bitter aftertaste. Among its many purported benefits, it's seen as both a digestive aid and a sleep aid. Barley tea can be enjoyed in many ways: hot, cold, sweetened or not. In Korea, sometimes corn is added to sweeten the mix.

Basil Tea: Not to be confused with "Holy Basil" tea (see Tulsi Tea on

page 83), this infusion is made
with just about any type of dried
basil, from Italian basil to sweet
basil to cinnamon basil. Earthy
and aromatic, it can be amped up
with a little black tea or flavored
with honey and/or citrus. This tea
is said to be good for oral health.

Brahmi Tea: This tea is made
from the dried or fresh leaves
of the bacopa monnieri plant, a
succulent-like wetland perennial,
native to Asia. Brahmi, nicknamed

"herb of grace," is said to boost brain function and reduce stress and anxiety. As a beverage, it has a singular, bittersweet flavor and natural cooling properties.

Borage Tea: Borage (rhymes with *porridge*) is an annual flowering herb, native to the Mediterranean. Its leaves are covered in tiny spines; boiling them softens them and makes them suitable for consumption. The tea has a cucumber-like flavor. Borage has long been used medicinally; in fact, ancient Greeks are said to have used it to ease melancholy.

Brown Rice Tea: The process of making this toasty tea goes like this: Wash and soak brown rice, roast it, then steep it in boiling water. Or, if that's too hard, you can buy preroasted and ready-to-steep rice kernels in the supermarket. The pale to golden-hued tea has a nutty, earthy flavor. Sometimes, actual tea (usually green) is added.

Buckwheat Tea: Despite the name, buckwheat is not a type of wheat at all; rather, it's a flowering plant that has grain-like seeds. To make this tea, the buckwheat seeds are husked, cooked, pan-fried, then steeped. Served hot or cold, Buckwheat tea is light yellow to golden in color with a nutty and toasty flavor. It is said to have anti-inflammatory and immune-boosting properties.

Butterfly Pea Tea: This tea does a cool trick: It turns bright blue when you add water! It's made with neither butterflies nor peas, but, rather, the dried buds of the vibrant blue butterfly pea wildflower. Despite the spectacular color, the flavor is quite subtle— earthy and vaguely chamomile-esque. It's the key ingredient in Color-Changing tea (page 122).

Chai Tea (Herbal): Chai is most commonly known as a milky tea drink, but it can also be a warming herbal tea mix. Herbal Chai tea mixes may vary but will often employ rooibos or tulsi instead of a black tea base, surrounded by a supporting cast of spices, such as cardamom, cinnamon, cloves, ginger, and/or star anise. Milk and sugar optional.

Chamomile Tea: One of the most famous herbal teas! This tea is made with the dried flowers of the chamomile plant, a flowering herb that's related to daisies and asters. The golden-hued tea, which has a subtle minty-flowery flavor and natural, almost honey-like sweetness, is known for its calming properties and is said to promote relaxation and sleep.

Chicory Root Tea: Made with dried pieces of chicory root, Chicory Root tea yields a brew with a coffee-like color and a bitter yet warm flavor that resembles coffee but has no caffeine. It's sometimes cut with coffee, but it can also be enjoyed as a coffee alternative or a stand-alone tea that promotes healthy digestion.

Chocolate Tea: Chocolate and tea are both great—but are they better together? If you're a chocolate lover, it may be a question worth exploring. Chocolate tea may include brews with actual pieces of chocolate or tea steeped with hot chocolate mix, but it may also be a toasty tea infusion made with cocoa nibs or even steeped cacao pod husks.

Chrysanthemum Tea: It's a treat to watch this tea steep: Pour hot water over food-grade chrysanthemum buds and watch the aquatic show as they unfurl. (You can get Chrysanthemum tea in bags, too, but where's the fun in that?) Despite the fact that it has literal flowers in it, this sunny-colored tea doesn't taste overly "flowery," but has a subtle, earthy sweetness.

Cinnamon Tea: This fragrant tea is a cinch to make: Simply pour hot water over a cinnamon stick (or sticks) and let it get nice and spicy. It will become more reddish and darker in color the longer you steep, and the flavor will become more pronounced. This tea is said to be a powerful, antioxidant-rich anti-inflammatory and it may relieve menstrual cramps.

Coffee Cherry Tea: Did you know that the coffee plant bears a type of fruit? It's called cascara or coffee cherries. (Coffee beans are actually the seeds of the fruit.) This slightly caffeinated tea is made with the fruit's dried skins. Despite the name, the brick-colored beverage tastes nothing like coffee and is decidedly fruit-like. It's an uplifting and purportedly cognitive-boosting tea.

Corn Tea: How corny! Commonly consumed in Korea under the name *oksusu-cha* (not to be confused with Corn Silk tea, which is also a thing), Corn tea is made by boiling dried and roasted corn kernels until the water turns yellow. At that point, the corn is strained, leaving you with a naturally sweet and super-hydrating beverage that's packed with vitamin C.

Cota Tea: Also called Navajo, Hopi, or Zuni tea, this tea is made with the leaves of the cota plant, a relative of the sunflower, that grows in the American Southwest. Cota has been used medicinally for hundreds of years by Indigenous peoples and is said to cure everything from a sour stomach to colds. It makes an earthy, mild, slightly grassy-tasting tea.

Dandelion Tea: This tea isn't made with dandelion flowers, but rather roasted pieces of the dandelion plant's root. The brewed beverage tastes and looks a lot more like coffee than a flowery herbal tea. For that reason, naturally caffeine-free dandelion tea is commonly used

as a coffee substitute and sometimes even marketed as "dandelion coffee."

Elderflower Tea: The elder tree
isn't just ornamental—its creamy,
highly aromatic flowers make
for a soothing tea that doubles
as a cough remedy. Elderflower

tea can be made with fresh elderflowers (no leaves; they're bitter!), when they are in summertime bloom, or with dried flowers. Elderflower tea is yellow with a clean, crisp flavor and a touch of floral sweetness.

Eucalyptus Tea: This tea may smell like Vicks VapoRub, but, happily, it doesn't taste like it. It's made by steeping dried eucalyptus leaves, typically from Australian eucalyptus. The resulting tea has a pale green color and a fresh, woodsy scent and flavor. Eucalyptus tea is often used as a home remedy to treat cold and flu symptoms.

Fennel Tea: Fun fact: During the Middle Ages, people hung fennel on their doors to ward off evil spirits. While that custom has fallen out of favor, fennel is still popular in the culinary arena. Fennel tea is made from the dried seeds of the fennel plant;

it has a sweet, licorice-like aroma and flavor, and is said to aid in digestion.

Ginger Tea: Spicy and soothing at the same time, this simple tea is made by simmering chunks of fresh gingerroot in water.

While the color of the tea is light, the flavor can be quite powerful, depending on how much ginger you use and how long you simmer it. This tea is said to boost the "inner fire" of digestion and reduce inflammation.

Gingko Tea: Did you know that the gingko tree is one of the oldest living tree species? Its singular fan-shaped leaves are perhaps best-known as an ingredient in memory-boosting supplements, but they also make a mighty fine tea. The infused dry leaves yield a gold-green-hued tea with an earthy, woodsy flavor that is often combined with citrus for an invigorating brew.

Ginseng Tea: This herbal tea is made from the dried root of the ginseng plant, which has long been used as a dietary supplement to boost energy and vitality. As a tea, it has a warming and earthy flavor with a touch of bitterness. In Korea, where the tea is particularly popular, it's often served with honey.

Goji Tea: Goji berries, also known as wolfberries, are a native Chinese sweet-sour superfood that have been touted for their ability to promote everything from weight loss to longevity. They also make for a super tea. Goji tea is typically made with dried berries, which are sweeter than their fresh counterparts, yielding a smooth-sipping beverage with a fruity and slightly sour aftertaste.

Gotu Kola Tea: Legend has it that a tai chi master lived over two hundred years as a result of taking gotu kola—no wonder it's called the "longevity herb"! Gotu Kola tea is made with dried or fresh leaves of the plant, which is part of the parsley family. The infusion has a mellow, fresh flavor with a light to deep green color.

Hemp Tea: This greenish-brown brew is made with leaves or flower buds from the *Cannabis sativa* plant. While it may contain trace amounts of THC, it's probably not enough to get you high. However, it does contain CBD, a purportedly health-boosting compound that could make you feel relaxed. Its earthy, slightly bitter flavor is an acquired taste.

Hibiscus Tea: Pretty in pink! The first thing you'll notice about this tea, which is made from the petals and other parts of the flowering hibiscus plant, is its rich, ruby hue. The second thing? The flavor. Hibiscus tea has a cranberry-esque tartness that makes you pucker up in all the right ways. This tea can be served hot or cold.

Honeybush Tea: This tea is sweet as honey, but it doesn't actually contain any. It comes from the dried leaves of the honeybush, an African shrub named for its flowers' honey-like aroma. Honeybush is in the same family as rooibos, and, like its cousin, it yields a tea with a reddish tint and a mellow, sweet flavor. Honeybush tea purportedly has cancer-fighting properties.

Honeysuckle Tea: Love the scent of honeysuckles? Give this tea a try. Made from either fresh or dried honeysuckle flowers, this pale green brew has a floral scent and a sweet flavor that almost tastes presweetened and is great consumed hot or cold. Honeysuckle is said to support respiratory health and may help clear airways if you have a cold.

Hops Tea: Hops: They're not just for making beer! Turns out, you can pour hot water over dried hop cones and make yourself a calming and sleep-promoting tea.

Visually, it looks like green tea and has a herbaceous and slightly bitter flavor. It's common to soften the flavor with another sweeter tea, like chamomile, or by adding honey.

Iceland Moss Tea: If you're a fan of woodsy flavors, give this tea a try! Despite the name, Iceland moss, which resembles moss and grows in Northern countries, including Iceland, isn't true moss. It's actually a hardy Alpine lichen (a plant form that's the result of an algae-fungi

fusion) that is typically ground
into a powder to make tea. The
flavor is, well, mossy, but that's
not necessarily why people drink
it. Iceland Moss tea, is often used
as a cold and cough remedy.

Jiaogulan Tea: This tea is made from the fresh or dried leaves of the jiaogulan plant, a climbing vine from Asia. The plant is related to cucumbers and melons, whose flavor shines through in this tea; it has a bittersweet, grassy, cucumber-like flavor. This is a popular herbal substitute for green tea. Sometimes called the "immortality herb," jiaogulan is used as an overall immune booster.

Jujube Tea: This tea isn't made with rainbow-colored candy but nature's candy! Jujubes are red dates that are native to Southeast Asia. The tea is made by steeping dried jujubes, which impart to the beverage both a distinctive red color and a delicious sweet-tart flavor with hints of cinnamon. It is often prepared with ginger. Jujube tea is said to alleviate menstrual cramps.

Kava Tea: This relaxation tonic of a tea is made from the ground roots of kava kava, which is part of the same family as black pepper. *Kava* comes from the word *awa*, which means "bitter" in Tongan and Marquesan. The flavor takes getting used to—some say it's sort of like muddy water. However, its calming qualities may motivate you to develop a taste for it.

Kelp Tea: Yep: Seaweed tea is a thing. This East Asian tea is made by infusing kelp—a large greenish-brown seaweed that is either dried or ground—in hot water. The resulting tea is some-what soup-like, with plenty of umami (a rich, savory flavor). Kelp tea is brimming with vitamins and minerals and it's one of the few teas that is rich in iodine.

Kuding Tea: Also referred to as "Bitter Nail tea" or just "Needle tea," this herbal infusion is made from the leaves of the *Ilex kaushue* plant, a relative of holly. Its nicknames come from its bitter taste and the fact that the leaves are rolled into needle-like shapes. Kuding tea is said to be an effective weight-loss aid.

Labrador Tea: Labrador tea is actually the name of the plant that this tea comes from (though nobody calls the infusion "Labrador tea tea"), a hardy plant related to rhododendron that grows in North America. Athabaskans and other Indigenous peoples favor this pine- and eucalyptus-flavored brew as a medicinal beverage for sore throats and chest ailments.

Lavender Tea: Pretty in . . . purple? This tea is made by infusing the buds of the lavender plant, which sometimes impart a slight purple hue. Even more attention-getting is its aromatic fragrance.

Flavor-wise, the tea is earthy, floral, slightly sweet, and has a touch of mint (lavender is in the same family). This tea is said to promote relaxation and sleep.

Lemon Balm Tea: Despite the name, lemon balm is not closely related to the citrus fruit—in fact, it's more closely related to mint. The plant has distinctly mint-like leaves that give off a lemon-like scent when rubbed. The dried leaves are used to make this uplifting and soothing tea, which has a golden color, a lemony scent, and a mild, mint-lemon flavor.

Lemongrass Tea: Once again, not related to lemon. Lemongrass is actually a type of flowering, grass-like plant from Asia that is named for its distinctive yet subtle citrus flavor that also has hints of ginger. Lemongrass has long been considered a staple of Asian cuisine. The tea—which is made from either dried or fresh lemongrass—is said to aid digestion and boost immunity.

Lemon Peel Tea: When life gives you lemons, make Lemon Peel tea! This tart tea is made by boiling plain or sugared lemon peels until they soften and release their essential oils into the water. The resulting infusion has a lemony flavor but a lower pucker factor than lemon juice, and is said to eliminate gas and improve digestion.

Licorice Tea: Did you know that *licorice* means "sweet herb" in Chinese? The legume (yes, it's a legume!) is native to western Asia, North Africa, and southern Europe. Its root, which is famed as a flavoring for candy and food products, also makes for a smooth-sipping tea with a golden color and a singular, sweet, and earthy aroma and flavor.

Lotus Tea: Lotus tea can refer to any number of infusions from the lotus plant—the embryos, leaves, fruit, roots, and seeds. Sometimes it's even made with a whole fresh flower, which symbolizes the "blossoming" of Buddhist enlightenment. Lotus infusions have a rich, floral aroma

and a flavor with touches of anise
and Asian pear. Lotus tea has
antioxidant properties and may
fight inflammation.

Marshmallow Root Tea:

Marshmallows were named
after their resemblance to the
marshmallow plant's blooms,
but this tea tastes nothing like
candy! It's made from the dried
or fresh root of the plant and
has an earthy and woodsy flavor.
Marshmallow Root tea has been

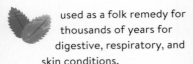 used as a folk remedy for thousands of years for digestive, respiratory, and skin conditions.

Moroccan Mint Tea: This tea is made with a distinctive type of mint that is cultivated in mountainous areas of Morocco. It's a social drink in Northwest Africa and parts of the Middle East, where it's usually served very sweet. As a stand-alone herbal tea, it has a more herbaceous flavor and a more subtle mint flavor than your typical mint tea.

Moringa Tea: As a plant, the fast-growing and drought-resistant moringa tree is occasionally viewed as invasive. But, as a consumable, its leaves (usually dried or powdered) are considered a superfood; it's brimming with nutrients, including four times the calcium of cow's milk. Moringa tea has an earthy, bitter yet slightly sweet flavor, sometimes compared to spirulina, matcha, and spinach.

Mugwort Tea: Mugwort tea might sound like a drink fit for a hobbit, but it's actually a real-life medicinal tea that is made from the leaves of the mugwort plant, which is native to Europe, Asia, and Africa. Flavor-wise, Mugwort tea is bittersweet with subtle anise undertones. Among its selling points? Mugwort tea contains

a chemical called thujone that
may stimulate the uterus and
promote lucid dreaming.

Mushroom Tea: Mushroom tea
is (and tastes) just like what it
sounds like: mushrooms (fresh,
dried, or powdered), infused
in hot water. While this category may include psychedelic
mushrooms, it can also include
non-trippy varieties, such
as chaga mushrooms, which
are said to have anti-cancer

properties; reishi mushrooms, which boost immunity; and lion's mane mushrooms, which may improve cognitive health and reduce anxiety.

Nettle Tea: Nettle tea is made with leaves from the stinging nettle plant, a perennial herb with stinging hairs that can irritate the skin. Happily, the tea doesn't sting, but it does pack a flavor punch—a distinctive, almost spinach-y taste with hints of pepper. Some consider it a spring tonic that wakes up the body from winter hibernation.

Olive Leaf Tea: The olive plant is a real jack-of-all-trades: Not only are its branches and fruit legendary, but its leaves make a delicious and uplifting tea. The long, silver-green leaves are pro- cessed much like tea leaves, and the tea tastes somewhat like an herbaceous green tea. Olive leaf is a natural antioxidant and anti-inflammatory that may help fight yeast and viral infections.

Omija Tea: Omija, or magnolia berry, is nicknamed "five-flavor berry," and this tea delivers on that promise. Slow-simmered dried berries make for a tea that's salty, sweet, bitter, sour, and pungent all at once, with a vibrant red color to boot. The tea is often

sweetened with honey and is
said to lower blood pressure and
promote detoxification.

Osmanthus Tea: Hailing from Guilin
("Forest of Sweet Osmanthus")
in southern China, the osmanthus plant features dainty and
highly fragrant flowers that
are used to make this tea. The
infusion has a trademark sweet-
sour flavor with apricot undertones. (Fun fact: Osmanthus is
also used to flavor beer and has

been featured in Pepsi products.) Osmanthus tea is said to
promote good skin tone and
detoxification.

Peppermint Tea: When most people
think of mint tea, they think of

peppermint tea. Technically, peppermint is a hybrid of two mint species—water mint and spearmint (the latter is another popular herbal tea). Peppermint is the "mintiest" of mint teas, owing to its higher concentration of menthol. This tea is calming yet invigorating, breath-freshening, and can be enjoyed hot or iced.

Persimmon Leaf Tea: Persimmon trees aren't just for fruit—their leaves can be used to make tea, too. Persimmon leaves are processed following some of the steps used in traditional tea production and these leaves make for a tea that's mellow and earthy but with a touch of tartness. Persimmon Leaf tea is commonly used to boost metabolism, aid in digestion, and improve blood flow.

Pine Needle Tea: Strain this tea carefully before you drink

it—it's made from the needles of pine trees. The infusion smells strongly of pine, but, happily, it doesn't taste like a cleaning product. Rather, it has a subtle, slightly astringent pine flavor that pairs beautifully with citrus and mint. This tea is packed with immune-boosting vitamin C.

Ranovola Tea: Burnt rice tea is a Malagasy specialty that kills two birds with one stone. First, it makes easy work of the rice crust that forms in the bottom of the pot while cooking. Second, it gives boiled water (a necessity for clean drinking water in some areas) a nice, toasty flavor. This golden-hued tea is said to be super-hydrating and good for digestion.

Raspberry Leaf Tea: This tea contains no fruit; it's actually made

from the leaves of the red raspberry plant. While it gives off a
fruit-like aroma, the flavor is a lot
more like full-bodied black tea,
although it contains no caffeine.
The plant is sometimes referred
to as the "woman's herb," and
Raspberry Leaf tea is said to
relieve premenstrual symptoms
and may help induce labor during
pregnancy.

Rooibos Tea: This tea comes from
the leaves of *Aspalathus linearis*,

a South African shrub in the legume family. It caught on when Dutch settlers dubbed it *rooibos* ("red bush") and began to drink it as a substitute for traditional tea. Naturally caffeine-free and antioxidant-rich, Rooibos tea has a brick-red color and a robust yet gentle flavor that's sweet and a little nutty.

Rose Tea: This romantic tea is made with dried rose petals or buds, often from *Rosa* *damascena*, the fluffy pink rose that's used to make rose oil, rose-water, and perfume. The flavor is sophisticated—floral, with hints of strawberry, apples, or even almonds (all part of the same family as roses). Rose tea is said to reduce anxiety and may relieve menstrual cramps.

Rose Hip Tea: Did you know that certain types of roses have "accessory fruits"? That's what rose hips are—small, berry-like fruits that grow below rose petals. They can be eaten or dried and infused into a lovely rosy-red tea. Unlike Rose tea, which is quite floral-tasting, Rose Hip tea has a sweet-tart flavor that is almost like a gentler Hibiscus tea.

Rosemary Tea: Rosemary is mostly considered a culinary herb, but you can also infuse it (fresh or dried) to make tea. The golden-hued brew has a distinctive rosemary aroma, but the flavor is subtle, with hints of lemon and mint (rosemary is part of the mint family). Rosemary has a warming and relaxing effect; studies show it may improve memory and stimulate the central nervous system.

Sage Tea: This aromatic infusion is made with the leaves of common sage, a culinary and medicinal herb in the mint family. It has a musky, minty flavor with a slightly bitter aftertaste and is frequently combined with a supporting flavor like mint or lemon. Sage is said to improve fertility, reduce menopausal symptoms, and enhance oral health.

Sakura Tea: Cherry blossom season is a big deal in Japan. While the season is short, the blossoms can be pickled in a preservative vinegar solution so they can be enjoyed all year round as a flavoring or as an herbal tea. Sakura ("Cherry Blossom") tea is made by steeping the preserved cherry blossoms in water and has an unusual, sweet-sour flavor.

Spearmint Tea: What differentiates spearmint tea from peppermint? While both relaxing teas are made from dried mint leaves, spearmint has a lot less naturally occurring menthol, about 0.5 percent versus 40 percent in pepper-mint. The result? Spearmint tea is a more subtle, sweeter, and smoother version of Peppermint tea. In addition to freshening the breath, spearmint is an antioxidant, an anti-inflammatory, and a digestive aid.

St. John's Wort Tea: St. John's wort is a native European shrub that flowers around a midsummer celebration called St. John's Day;

hence the name. Its flowers
have been used medicinally for
thousands of years, including as
tea. The infusion has a somewhat
bitter flavor; some love it, others tolerate it for its purported
benefits—St. John's Wort tea
is said to ease symptoms of
depression.

Tulsi Tea: Tulsi, also known as
"holy basil," is an aromatic herb
that has been used in religious,
spiritual, and healing practices

for thousands of years. Its dried leaves can be enjoyed as a stand-alone infusion or as the base for herbal tea mixes. This stress-relieving tea has a semisweet flavor with a touch of spiciness that has echoes of mint, clove, and anise.

Turmeric Tea: This singular, sunny-hued tea is made with the fresh, dried, or powdered root of the *Curcuma longa* plant, a member of the ginger family native

to India and Southeast Asia.
Curcumin, the same compound
that gives the tea its color,
also has anti-inflammatory and
immune-boosting properties and
is said to reduce brain plaque.
Turmeric tea has an earthy yet
spicy flavor.

Valerian Root Tea: Relaxation is
the name of the game with
this infusion. Valerian Root tea
is made with the roots of the
valerian plant, a flowering herb

native to Europe and parts of Asia, which has a long history of use as a sedative. The tea's earthy and slightly sweet flavor aren't appealing to everyone, so it's frequently mixed with other herbs.

Yaupon Tea: Also called "Cassina," this tea is made from the yaupon plant, a type of holly that's related to yerba mate. Like its relative, it contains caffeine; each cup contains about one-third the caffeine of a cup of coffee. It was once the favored pick-me-up of Indigenous North Americans, who called it "black drink." Flavor-wise, it has an earthy and sometimes grassy taste.

Yerba Mate Tea: This caffeinated South American tea, made from the dried leaves and stems of the *Ilex paraguariensis* plant (part of the holly family), is a real powerhouse—as strong as coffee but with all the health benefits of tea. Plus, it's served in a really cool, gourd-like container with a special metal straw to filter the leaf debris. Devotees love the strong, vegetal, bitter flavor.

Tea Drinks

Once upon a time, some genius had the idea to add milk and sugar to tea. Ever since, people have been adding a little bit of this and that to create one-of-a-kind tea drinks. Ranging from refreshing iced tea to grassy-green matcha lattes to tea with

cheesy froth on top, here are
some tea-rific drinks from
around the world.

Arnold Palmer: Sweet fusion!
This refreshing and (usually)
nonalcoholic bev is made with
iced tea and lemonade. It takes
its name from professional
golfer Arnold Palmer, who
popularized the drink; he is said
to have favored a ratio of three
parts unsweetened tea to one
part lemonade. The "Winnie

Palmer" (named for Arnold's first wife) features sweet tea and lemonade.

Bubble Tea: Bubble tea, or boba tea, is a tea drink that is served accompanied by chewy balls of tapioca. The tea base may be black tea, green tea, or oolong, served with or without milk. Originally created in the 1980s, the custom has become an international sensation; in the United States, you can celebrate National Bubble Tea Day on April 30.

Cheese Tea: Tea with cheese? Believe it. Also called "Milk Cap tea" or "Cheese Mousse tea," this cheesy confection of a drink is made by whipping cream cheese, confectioners' sugar, and milk into a thick, foam-like topping for black or green tea. This tea has caught on across Asia and in the

United States, where it's often served at bubble tea shops.

Hong Kong Milk Tea: The ingredients (black tea and evaporated and/or sweetened condensed milk) aren't the most interesting thing about this sweet tea drink. Rather, it's the exacting process, which involves straining the tea through a stocking-like filter (hence the nickname "Pantyhose tea"). In 2017, the unique technique used to make this drink was officially declared one of the intangible cultural heritages (ICHs) of China.

Horchata Lojana: Horchata Lojana is a bright pink herbal tea drink from Ecuador's Loja Province that's made with dozens of herbs and flowers, plenty of sugar, and sometimes even a little aloe vera. Is it the secret to longevity? Residents seem to think so: The area is called the Valley of Longevity for its many residents who pass the hundred-year mark.

Iced Tea: Iced tea is just what it sounds like: hot tea that's been put on ice to create a refreshing cool beverage. Its origins

are hazy, but it's said to have been popularized in the United States at the 1904 World's Fair in St. Louis. The timing was right: The weather was hot, the cold tea sold fast, and refreshed fairgoers helped pop-ularize it widely.

Irani Chai: First brought to India by Persian immigrants in the nineteenth century, this tea drink really took off in a big way in Hyderabad, a city in the northern part of southern India. The heavy-handed spice mix and extreme creaminess, thanks to either evaporated or sweetened condensed milk, make it distinct from Masala Chai.

Jun: You could think of Jun as Kombucha's cousin. In terms of its preparation, it's actually quite similar—but instead of black tea, it's usually made with green tea, and it's typically made with honey instead of sugar to kick-start the fermentation process. The resulting beverage is a little smoother and sweeter than Kombucha but with similar health benefits.

Kashmiri Chai: The first thing you'll notice about this popular Kashmiri beverage is its creamy rose hue. It's the result of boiling tea leaves with baking soda, which reacts with their chlorophyll and turns them a deep crimson color. The mix is then combined with milk and spices to make the signature "pink tea" that is often served as a midday treat.

Kombucha: Kombucha is a fermented tea drink made by combining tea (usually black) and a little sugar with a SCOBY (technically, a "symbiotic colony of bacteria and yeast"; informally, a horror-movie-looking gob of goo). The mixture is fermented for days or even weeks and flavorings may be added before serving. The resulting vinegar-y, sweet-and-sour drink is said to improve digestion and well-being.

Ladakh Chai: Butter me up! The drink of choice in Leh—a high-desert city in the Himalayas—is a buttery beverage sometimes called Gur Gur Chai. First, tea, baking soda, and salt are combined in an urn called a samovar, then butter and milk are added in a churn called a gur gur. As with Kashmiri chai, the baking soda causes a reaction that tints the drink pink.

London Fog: Talk about a cozy cup! The London Fog is a latte-esque drink made with Earl Grey tea, steamed milk, and vanilla syrup. Despite the name, it wasn't created in Britain but rather British Columbia. As the story goes, a

pregnant woman in Vancouver
who was avoiding coffee
ordered it frequently and sug-
gested it widely—eventually, the
trend caught on.

Masala Chai (Chai Tea Latte):
Masala Chai means "Mixed
Spiced tea" in Hindi and that's
just what this Indian beverage
is: a mix of black tea, milk, and
a mélange of herbs and spices,
commonly cardamom and
ginger, but the mix may also

include cinnamon, cloves, nutmeg, star anise, peppercorns . . . the list goes on and on. Masala Chai has become an international sensation and inspired the Western spin-off, the chai latte.

Matcha Latte: This mixed tea drink shares the key characteristics of a latte—milky liquid topped with foam—but it's made with matcha powder instead of espresso, which gives it a vibrant green hue. Served either hot or cold,

Matcha Lattes are often made with Culinary-Grade Matcha, which tastes more bitter and grassy than Ceremonial-Grade Matcha. For that reason, Matcha Lattes are often sweetened.

Peanut Tea: Think peanut butter is just for sandwiches? Think again. In Ethiopia, it's common-place to drink an infusion called Peanut tea that may or may not include tea leaves. To make it, simply boil water, add peanut butter until it's reached your desired consistency, and sweeten to taste. It sort of tastes like drinking a peanut butter cookie—not such a bad thing at all.

Seven-Layer Tea: Taste the rainbow! This distinctive tea beverage resembles an earth-toned rainbow with pretty layers of cream, brown, red, and green. It was created by a clever

Bangladeshi tea shop owner
who figured out that different
combos of spices, tea leaves,
and milk types could be used
to create a multilayered drink.
While the original recipe is pro-
prietary, the concept has been
copied globally.

Sweet Tea:
Southern-style
sweet tea isn't
just tea with
sugar. It's a

labor of love, often made in big batches. First, sugar and water are boiled down to make a thin syrup. Then, tea bags are steeped in the sugar slurry until the water cools. This super-strong sweet tea concentrate can be diluted with water to taste and is a fixture in many Southern fridges.

Tea Frappé: A frappé (pronounced fra-PAY) is an iced beverage that has been shaken or blended with ice to produce a frothy and refreshing drink. When you add tea, it's sort of like a tea milk-shake! Two common types are a Thai Tea Frappé, made with black tea and sweetened condensed milk, and a Green Tea Frappé, made with matcha and milk.

Tea Punch: The first known mention of punch was in 1632 (in correspondence from an employee of the British East India Company), right around the time that tea was becoming popular in Europe, so it's likely that the two were combined early. Today, Tea Punch can cover a pretty wide range for multi-ingredient beverages, from Bourbon Tea Punch to (Virgin) Tea and Fruit Punch.

Teh Tarik: Considered the "unofficial national drink of Malaysia," Teh Tarik ("Pulled tea") is named for its showy preparation, which involves pouring black

tea and sweetened condensed
milk between two vessels at a
high height to agitate the liquid
and create a thick, frothy top
while simultaneously cooling
it to a drinkable temperature.
It's popular in coffee shops and
markets and even in surrounding
countries.

Thai Tea: If you've been to a Thai restaurant, you've probably seen this signature beverage—a mixture of potent Ceylon tea combined with sweetened condensed milk, served either hot or over ice. Since the tea and milk have different weights, it may have a lovely two-tone appearance. It's a popular drink, available from street vendors in Thailand and across Southeast Asia.

Tibetan Butter Tea: This rich and somewhat savory beverage is made with strong tea, butter (often yak butter), and salt, churned together. It's said that its high caloric load helps maintain energy in the cold mountainous regions where it's commonly quaffed, but it also serves as a digestive aid and can help soothe chapped lips.

Unusual
Teas

There are thousands of types of tea out there. Many may be classified by type; others simply defy categorization. This section is dedicated to the latter category. These unusual, exotic, and

sometimes downright strange teas are worth knowing about.

Beef Tea: Nice to *meat* you! Recipes for beef tea dating back to the 1700s involve boiling down a cut of meat with water and a sprinkle of salt. This savory "tea" was viewed as a vitality-boosting and warming health tonic. Perhaps you'd feel more comfortable eating it with a spoon: Beef tea recipes bear

more than a passing resemblance
to beef broth recipes.

Bug-Bitten Tea: Bugs aren't always the enemy of tea crops. Bug-bitten teas are made when tea plants aren't treated with insecticides, which invites bugs to come snack. The tiny bug bites trigger the release of biosynthetic building blocks called terpenes, which give the tea a sweet, honey-like flavor. Dongfang Meiren ("Eastern Beauty" tea) is an example.

Color-Changing Tea: The effect is magical—tea that turns color right before your eyes! But actually, it's just a science trick that involves manipulating the pH levels of Butterfly Pea tea (page 25). All you have to do is add an acidic ingredient (often lemon); the bright blue tea will turn purple in mere moments, which makes for a great tea party parlor trick.

Flowering Teas: Tea and a show!
Also called "Blooming teas,"
these visually stunning, lovely
tea sensations are made with tea
buds wrapped around a flower
or flowers that have been tightly
packed and sewn by hand into
shapes like spheres or rosettes.
When hot water is added, the
little tea-and-flower nuggets
slowly unfurl, almost like slow-mo
fireworks in your cup.

Panda Dung Tea: Don't worry—it's not as gross as it sounds. This tea is made using panda dung as a fertilizer—an eco-friendly cultivation method that is said to retain more nutrients and yield a fragrant and smooth tea. But it doesn't come cheap. When this tea first came to market, it was the world's most expensive tea— sixteen cups' worth cost about $3,500.

Pickled Tea: Would you eat tea? In Myanmar, lahpet, or Pickled tea, is a common food item. To make it, tea leaves are subjected to a three-part fermentation process that results in a pulpy pickled mixture so beloved that it inspired a saying: "Of all the fruit, the mango's the best; of all the meat, pork's the best; and of all the leaves, lahpet's the best."

Black, Oolong, Green, Yellow, White Tea & More

JESSIE OLESON MOORE
ILLUSTRATED BY JESSIE FORD

PHILADELPHIA

RP Minis®
Hachette Book Group
1290 Avenue of the Americas, New York, NY 10104
www.runningpress.com
@Running_Press

Printed in China

First Edition: March 2024

Published by RP Minis, an imprint of Hachette Book Group, Inc.
The RP Minis name and logo is a registered trademark of
Hachette Book Group, Inc.

Running Press books may be purchased in bulk for business,
educational, or promotional use. For more information, please
contact your local bookseller or the Hachette Book Group
Special Markets Department at Special.Markets@hbgusa.com.

The publisher is not responsible for websites (or their content)
that are not owned by the publisher.

Library of Congress Control Number: 2023939504

ISBN: 978-0-7624-8515-4

HH

10 9 8 7 6 5 4 3 2 1

CONTENTS

BLACK TEA . . . 13

A simple cup of tea is far
from a simple matter.

—MARY LOU HEISS

Black Tea

B lack tea is arguably the most famous and factually the most consumed tea in the entire world. All black teas are made from the *Camellia sinensis* plant and are oxidized, or exposed to oxygen, to kick-start a chemical reaction that

darkens the leaves and gives
the finished brews their
distinctive, bold flavor.

While the first black teas
were produced in China and
India, tea plants have since
been cultivated in countless
other regions, from Sri Lanka
to the Kenyan foothills to
the United States. Different
growing conditions and
nuances in processing make

for an incredible array of black
teas out there to taste and
consume. Here are just a few
to discover.

American Black Tea: Chinese tea plants were brought to America in the 1700s, but it took years for tea-growing operations to thrive. Even today, American tea growers are few and far between. American Classic is a famous example of 100 percent USA-grown American black tea, produced by the Charleston Tea Garden, which was founded in the 1800s. The tea is described as smooth and fresh.

Assam Black Tea: Assam black tea refers to tea produced in the Assam region of northeastern India, one of the largest tea-producing areas of the world and one of the few areas of the world that is known to have native tea plants. Assam black teas are known for their malty, brisk flavor, which is favored for "breakfast" tea mixes.

Azorean Black Tea: São Miguel, the main island of the Portuguese archipelago known as the Azores Islands, is home to the only commercial tea-growing region in Europe. The temperate climate with regular rainfall is ideal for producing black teas that are said to echo the flavor of Ceylon teas, with a bright and sometimes even creamy texture.

Black Matcha: While "true" matcha is made with green tea, the same process of grinding leaves into a fine powder can also be done with black tea. Some consider black matcha a marketing ploy to sell dust left over from processing black tea leaves; others love the potent flavor, which varies depending on the type of ground tea used in the formulation.

Ceylon Black Tea: Ceylon black teas are produced in Sri Lanka (formerly Ceylon). Initial cultivation of Chinese tea plants in Sri Lanka failed; production only began in earnest when plants from Assam were successfully cultivated. While different regions of the country yield different products, Ceylon black tea has a reputation for being bold, crisp, and slightly citrusy, with a lot of tannins.

Chai Black Tea: The most famous chai tea drink, masala chai, is made by simmering black tea, milk, and spices. However, black tea can also be infused with spices to create a flavorful loose-leaf or bagged tea variety that can be enjoyed with milk and/or sugar or without. Typically, the spice blend includes cardamom, cinnamon, cloves, ginger, and/or star anise.

Congou Tea: This tea from China's Fujian Province is said to have been one of the varieties tossed into Boston Harbor in 1773! The word *congou* refers to the "mastery" required to create this tea's signature thin, delicate strips without breaking the leaves. The finished brew is worth the fuss, with a fruity scent, medium body, and a smooth drinking quality.

Darjeeling Black Tea: Darjeeling black tea is a singular tea indeed. It comes from a Chinese tea plant, but it's grown in the foothills of the Himalayas in India. The unique growing conditions give the tea a light flavor that is less astringent than many other black teas. Darjeeling black tea is sometimes called "the Champagne of teas" owing to its muscat grape-like flavor.

Dian Hong Cha: Dian hong cha translates as "Yunnan red tea." (What is referred to as black tea in America and elsewhere is referred to as red tea in China.)

This is a traditional black tea grown in Yunnan Province, which has a bold aroma and a smooth flavor with a sweet aftertaste. Dian hong cha is frequently used in tea blends.

Earl Grey: The connection between this tea and its name-sake, Charles Grey, second Earl Grey and former British prime minister, is hazy. But we do know this: It's a black tea made with oil of bergamot, a type of citrus fruit. While the practice of flavoring tea with bergamot was viewed as a trick to make lesser-quality teas flashier, Earl Grey is now considered quite posh.

Earl Grey Variants: Earl Grey is so popular that it's inspired several spin-offs worth mentioning. First, there's Lady Grey, a trademarked variation made with a mélange of different citrus fruits. But that's not all. Earl Grey Crème is made with cornflower and vanilla; Russian Earl Grey is made with citrus peel and lemongrass; and French Earl Grey features rose petals.

English Breakfast Tea: There are many legends behind this tea blend's origin. One of the earliest states that in the 1700s, Queen Anne started swapping tea for the tradi-tional ale served with breakfast, and a tradition was born. Today, English Breakfast tea is typically a blend of Assam, Ceylon, and/or Kenyan tea. It has a rich, robust flavor that goes well with milk and sugar.

Irish Breakfast Tea: The Irish are said to prefer their tea like their whiskey—very strong. This robust blend—which is traditionally stronger than English Breakfast tea—is dominated by Assam tea, which gives the finished product a malty flavor. The tea can range from reddish to dark brown and is traditionally served with lots of milk and sugar.

Jasmine Black Tea: Black tea may be intense, but the sweet fragrance and flavor of jasmine can help soften it. Like its arguably more famous jasmine green tea counterpart, this flowery black tea is made according to a time-honored tradition of layering tea leaves and jasmine blooms several times to create a fresh, fragrant, and sweet brew.

Jiu Qu Hong Mei: This tea is a rarity in Zhejiang Province, which primarily produces green tea. Its name means "Nine Winding Red Plum," a reference to the tea's plum-like color and fruit-like aroma. Flavorwise, it has a mellow sweetness and a slightly dry finish. Fun fact: This tea was mentioned in the popular novel *A Magnificent Tree of the South* by Wang Zufeng.

Kangra Black Tea: Kangra is a small tea-growing region in the shadow of the Dhauladhar mountain range in northern India and is nicknamed "Valley of the Gods." The climate and soil conditions make for a distinctive black tea. Kangra black tea has a fruit-forward aroma and flavor and smooth sweet aftertaste that is more subtle than Darjeeling teas.

Keemun Tea: Meet one of the most famous Chinese black teas!

Keemun is produced in Qimen County of Anhui Province, a growing region near the Yellow Mountains and the Yangtze River. While there are countless variations of this tea, some of its key characteristics are its smoky-floral aroma and light, nonastringent, woodsy flavor with notes of cocoa.

Kenyan Black Tea: The first tea plants were only introduced to Kenya in the early 1900s, but it's become a powerhouse tea producer since then. The majority of Kenya's tea is grown in the nutrient-rich volcanic soil of the Kenyan highlands, where unique growing conditions give Kenyan black teas a distinctive, robust, brisk, and bright flavor.

Lapsang Souchong: As legend has it, this tea was created during the Qing dynasty (about 1644–1912) when residents of China's Wuyi region had to hastily abandon their tea-making process to avoid advancing soldiers; they roasted the leaves over pine wood and buried them in sacks in an attempt to salvage the harvest. Apparently, they liked the results—the singular, smoky-sweet tea is still hugely popular today.

Lychee Black Tea: This fragrant black tea is said to have become popular more than a thousand years ago during the Tang dynasty (about 618–907). It is made with lychee fruit peel, which is roasted with tea leaves to impart a tropical, honey-like flavor that lightens up bold black tea. The lychee peel may be included or filtered out before the tea is sold.

Nepali Black Tea: Himalayan tea-producing areas in China and Darjeeling are famous; Nepali tea is lesser-known but no less respectable. Given the growing region's proximity to Darjeeling, Nepali black tea bears more than a passing resemblance to Darjeeling tea with a fruit-forward aroma and smooth, nonastringent drinking quality, but tends to be less expensive.

New Zealand Black Tea: Tea production in New Zealand is fairly new and mainly limited to the Waikato area, a region that sits below Auckland. The growing conditions and abundant rainfall make for lush tea-growing conditions. While the region produces various types of tea, its black teas are noteworthy, with a full body and a sweet, honey-like finish.

Nilgiri Black Tea: Also called "Blue Mountain tea," Nilgiri tea is grown and processed in the mountainous Nilgiris district in southern India. The British first introduced Chinese tea plants to the area in the 1830s; two monsoon seasons and extended periods of fog and humidity are perfect for growing tea plants. Nilgiri black tea is aromatic, brisk, and full-bodied.

Russian Caravan: Despite the name, this tea blend is actually from China. It's named for the camel caravans that facilitated the international tea trade to Europe from China via Russia. During the months-long journey, the tea in tow took on a smoky flavor, thanks to nightly campfires. Today, the mix is typically Keemun and

Lapsang Souchong; the latter
imparts the signature smoky flavor.

Scottish Breakfast Tea: A Scottish tea
master is said to have developed
this tea in the late 1800s as an
alternative to English Breakfast
tea. Like other breakfast teas,
this is a black tea mix that often
includes Assam tea.
Some say Scottish
brews are extra-
strong to combat
the country's soft

water; true or not, it's typically stronger than its English and Irish counterparts.

Sikkim Black Tea: While it's relatively little-known, there's a small tea-growing region in the state of Sikkim, located in northeast India, between Bhutan and Nepal. The region's black teas are often compared to the more famous offerings from the nearby Darjeeling region, but are worth appreciating in their own right.

Sikkim black teas have a light, delicate, and malty flavor.

Turkish Black Tea: Turkey primarily produces black tea, which is grown in a northeastern region by the East Black Sea called Rize. It is either referred to as "Rize tea" or just simply "Turkish tea." Throughout the country, black tea is ubiquitous and typically served in small, tulip-shaped glasses. Turkish black tea has a bitter and astringent flavor and is almost always sweetened.

Yingde Hong: This Chinese black tea was developed in the 1950s using a cultivar developed with big-leaf plants imported from Yunnan. It caught on quickly and the Queen of England is said to have served Yingde Hong tea in 1963, which cemented its fame. The tea has a vivid amber-red color and a floral aroma with hints of citrus and caramel.

Oolong Tea

Most people think that oolong tea is a type of black tea. Nope! While both tea types are made according to a similar process, there are some important differences. The biggest one? Oxidation. While black teas are highly oxidized, oolong teas are only partly oxidized. The leaves might range in color from greenish to quite dark, and the flavor can lean more toward black or green tea territory, depending on how oxidized it is and how it's processed. There's a wide range of oolong flavors to discover— here are just a few.

Baozhong: This lightly oxidized tea falls somewhere between green tea and oolong, though it's usually categorized as the latter. The name means "Wrapped Kind," referring to a method of wrapping tea leaves in paper to dry. Technology has mostly killed the old-school process, but the leaves still have a signature twisted shape. Baozhong tea has a floral fragrance and a mild flavor.

Da-Hong Pao: The origins of this tea's flashiest nickname, "Big Red Robe," are hazy. What we do know is that it's one of the relatively few teas produced in the Wuyi mountains (nickname #2: "Wuyi Rock Tea"). The rolled leaves, which resemble tiny knots, make for a bright, yellow-orange infusion with a floral aroma and a long-lasting, sweet aftertaste.

Darjeeling Oolong: Surprise! The Darjeeling region doesn't just produce black teas. Darjeeling oolong tea has many of the hallmarks of a Darjeeling, like a muscat-grape aroma, but it also has the lingering floral notes that people crave in an oolong. It's considered a tea for connoisseurs who want to sample an oolong with a different terroir.

Dong Ding Oolong Tea: This popular oolong tea is grown in the rainy, mountainous Lugu region with plants from China's Wuyi

Mountains. It's made according to a very specific oxidation and roasting process that results in a rich, sweetly flavored tea that is suitable for all-day drinking.

Dongfang Meiren: Also called "Eastern Beauty," this is one of the most famous oolong teas. The secret behind its ambrosial aroma? Bugs. When the tea plant is bitten by insects, a chemical reaction occurs; combined with partial oxidation,

it gives the tea a distinctive,
honey-like flavor.

Po Shou: This tea is nicknamed
"Buddha's Hand," possibly
because it features unusually
large leaves that expand and
open like a hand when brewed,
or maybe due to its citrus scent
that calls to mind the fruit of
the same name. This oolong
originated in China and has a
soft, bright flavor, with notes
of plum.

Huang Jin Gui: This lightly oxidized oolong hails from the Anxi village of Fujian, China, a mountainous region with mineral-rich soil that produces highly sought-after teas. This tea is nicknamed "Golden Cassia," owing to the infusion's golden-yellow hue. It has a distinctive osmanthus fragrance (a type of flower that is also used to make herbal tea) and a light flavor.

Jin Xuan: This Taiwanese tea was developed in the early 1980s and is only made from tea plants grown at a very high altitude; these conditions plus partial oxidation impart a rich, creamy flavor with notes of butter and milk that gives the tea the nickname "Milk Oolong". Buy from a reputable source: Some manufacturers add flavorings to oolong tea to get that milky flavor.

Kenyan Oolong Tea: Calling all oolong lovers! Kenyan oolongs are few and far between, but well worth seeking out. Most of the country's oolongs are produced in the Great Rift Valley, an area with high altitude, volcanic soil, and plenty of rain. These conditions make for singular oolongs with a great variety of flavors, depending on oxidation level.

Mao Xie: This oolong from Anxi County, in China's Fujian Province, is lovingly referred to as "Hairy Crab," but don't worry— it doesn't taste like seafood. It's named for the tiny, downy hairs that cover its small, rounded leaves. This low-oxidized oolong has vegetal notes like a green tea, but with a fruit-like finish.

Phoenix Dan Cong Tea: This oolong is said to have been around for about nine hundred years. It is solely produced in the mountains of Guangdong Province, and some say these plants are the "mother" of all oolongs. Hallmarks of a true, high-quality Phoenix oolong include a fruit-like aroma and flavor, and the ability to withstand several steepings.

Tieguanyin: This is both a type of oolong tea and a tea cultivar that's named for Guanyin, the Chinese Goddess of Mercy (it's also called "Iron Goddess of

Mercy"). As such, Tieguanyin covers a lot of territory! As an oolong, it features leaves rolled into tight balls that can vary from nutty to fruity or vegetal in flavor.

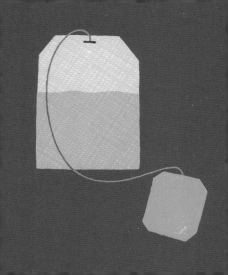

Green Tea

Y ou could think of green tea as the alternate-reality version of black tea. The leaves for both teas come from the same plant, but once they're picked, they part ways. Unlike black tea—which relies on oxidation for its rich, deep flavor—green tea is immediately heated to halt oxidation. Not only does this help the leaves retain their green color, but it also has a big effect on the flavor. Green tea has a much more vegetal and grassy flavor than robust black tea. It can also be more delicate: Green tea typically requires less steeping and can become quite bitter if steeped too long. Here are just a few green teas from around the globe.

Anji Bai Cha: The name translates as "Anji white tea," but it's actually a green tea, produced primarily in Anji County in China's Zhejiang Province. While the cultivar is said to be ancient, it was only discovered in the 1980s. The harvesting season is quite short and the highly prized leaves make for a tea that's sweet and thick, with plenty of umami (a rich, savory flavor).

Assam Green Tea: Assam is so well-known for its black teas that it may be surprising to learn that green teas are produced there, too. While the tea is not oxidized, it still has a distinct Assam personality. Like its black tea counterparts, Assam green teas are brisk, but with a smooth and savory green tea flavor.

Bancha: *Bancha* refers to Japanese green teas that come from the "second flush" or harvest after Sencha (page 84). There are many Bancha subgrades, all of which are considered lower-grade than Sencha. Bancha can be processed in a number of different ways—roasted or unroasted, smoked, or even fermented. The flavor may range from earthy to nutty or smoky.

Biluochun: This popular Chinese green tea is grown in the Dongting mountain region of Jiangsu Province. Its name means "Green Snail Spring," referring to the spring-harvested tea leaves that are rolled into a signature spiral shape. The tea is famous for its distinctive appearance and for its strong fruit-like aroma and flavor.

Ceylon Green Tea: Ceylon (now called Sri Lanka) is one of the biggest black tea producers in the world, but the country also produces exquisite green teas. The main types of green tea produced are gunpowder and Sencha-style teas. Primarily grown in the Uva region of Sri Lanka, using plants from Assam, Ceylon green teas have a full body and a nutty, sometimes even malty, flavor.

Chai Green Tea: Typically, chai tea is made with black tea. However, green tea can make for a great base for a flavorful infusion that may include aromatic spices like cinnamon, cloves, and cardamom. Green tea lends a completely different flavor profile to chai than black tea and can be enjoyed sans milk or prepared latte-style.

Chun Mee: This popular Chinese green tea is also known as "Precious Eyebrows," due to its bowed shape, which is the result of careful hand-rolling. It was originally produced in China's Jiangxi Province, but now it is grown elsewhere and has its own set of numbered grades. The golden infusion has a certain tartness; some say it has a plum-like flavor.

Darjeeling Green Tea: Black teas may be the darling of Darjeeling, but its green teas deserve respect, too. The unique growing conditions in the foothills of the Himalayas, combined with Chinese tea plants, makes for a green tea unlike any other—it has the muscat note that Darjeeling lovers know and love, but with the signature light and vegetal flavor of green tea.

Earl Grey Green Tea: Bergamot-scented Earl Grey proved so popular that enterprising tea producers decided to give it a go with green tea. Earl Grey

Green Tea, or sometimes just Earl Green, is made with green tea (often gunpowder) combined with oil of bergamot. While the idea is similar to traditional Earl Grey, green tea gives this tea a totally different character.

Genmaicha Green Tea: Genmaicha means "Brown Rice tea," and that's exactly what it is—Japanese green tea with roasted brown rice. Rice was originally added as a filler to reduce the price of the tea; this grassy, earthy, and popcorn-y tea is now internationally beloved. Wait, popcorn-y? Yep. Sometimes rice grains pop while roasting, and they resemble popped corn kernels in both appearance and flavor.

Gyokuro: Referred to as "Jade Dew," this is a high-quality and assertively caffeinated tea that is grown in the shade at least two weeks before harvesting. This method interrupts photosynthesis, which helps the leaves retain more chlorophyll, meaning a deeper green color and fewer tannins. The brewed tea has a rich, umami flavor.

Hawaiian Green Tea:
Fun fact: Tea giant Lipton once considered growing tea in Hawaii. They didn't move forward on this plan, but these days plenty of smaller-scale growing operations

take advantage of the rich, volcanic soil, particularly on the Big Island. Hawaii's green teas are worth seeking out for their sweet and clean grassy flavor.

Hojicha: This green tea from Kyoto has a calling card: Its leaves aren't merely heated but roasted over charcoal to prevent oxidation. The process imparts a smoky, earthy aroma and removes bitterness from the brew. Hojicha's smoky, roasty, and umami flavor makes it a popular and lower-caffeine coffee alternative.

Hyeonmi-Nokcha: While green tea combined with toasted rice is mostly thought of as a Japanese phenomenon, Korea produces a variety as well. *Hyeonmi-Nokcha*, which translates simply as "Brown Rice green tea," is made with steamed green tea leaves combined with toasted brown rice. Like Genmaicha, it has a nutty and toasty flavor.

Jasmine Green Tea: This aromatic infusion is one of the most famous scented green teas in China. Its production involves an elaborate infusion process where fresh jasmine blossoms are combined with tea leaves, a process that may be repeated several times to attain just the right balance. The flavor is subtle, with a slight honey-suckle-like sweetness and an intoxicating fragrance.

Kabusecha: *Kabusecha* means "Covered tea" and refers to any number of Japanese teas that follow a specific shade-grown process. Typically, they are covered for a shorter time than Gyokuro teas. These shade-grown leaves are mostly used to produce superior green teas with a distinctive flavor and aroma, though they can also be used to make black or oolong tea.

Konancha: This fine-textured Japanese green tea is made from

the specks of tea debris left
over from producing Gyokuro or
Sencha tea leaves. Technically,
it's a by-product, so it tends
to be less expensive. However,
since it's sometimes made
from high-grade tea leaves, it
may have a great flavor for the

value. It's frequently used for tea bags and served at sushi establishments.

Korean Green Tea: The majority of Korean green tea exports are produced on the volcanic island of Jeju in South Korea. The rich, volcanic soil and humid climate are perfect for growing tea. Korean green teas tend to be milder than Chinese green teas and can range in flavor from spring-y to rich and vegetal, depending on the harvest time and processing.

Kukicha: This tea, which is also called "Stem tea" or "Twig tea," is typically composed of leftover stems from Matcha or Sencha production. While it's considered a second-grade tea in some regards, it has some distinctive benefits: It's lower in caffeine than most green tea; it has a sweet, pleasing aroma; and a mild flavor that's suitable for all-day drinking.

Longjing Tea: As legend has it, residents of Longjing ("Dragon Well") Village in China's Zhejiang Province once believed that a dragon lived nearby. When the country fell into drought, they called upon the dragon to help. It began to rain soon after, and they named this tea in tribute to the dragon. Dragon Well tea has a vibrant green color and a brisk flavor.

Lu'an Melon Seed Green Tea: There's no actual melon in this famous

Chinese green tea—it's named for the shape of the tea leaves after processing, which appear elongated and flat, like a melon's seed. While many green teas are made with buds, this tea is made with the second leaf on the branch. The flavor is clean, smooth, and a little nutty.

Malawi Green Tea: Malawi is said to be home to the oldest tea bushes in Africa, which produce rare but elegant green teas.

While the region is best-known for robust black teas, small-scale farmers produce some excellent green teas that are simultaneously delicate and rich with vegetal, nutty, and a spring-like green flavor.

Mao Feng: *Mao feng* means "Fur Peak" and refers to the leaves with a fine coating of white hair that are used to make this famous Chinese green tea. One of the most renowned and traditional varieties is Huang Shan Mao Feng, which is composed only of buds and young leaves. It has a strong, refreshing flavor with floral notes.

Matcha

Matcha is the powdered green tea that is part of the Japanese tea ceremony. It's made from the same leaves used to make Gyokuro green tea, which are air-dried, deveined,

de-stemmed, and ground to a
vibrant green powder. Matcha
can vary in flavor from sweet
to deep and slightly astringent,
depending on its grade. See
pages 82–83 for two key grades.

Ceremonial-Grade Matcha: This is the specific type of Matcha that is prepared and frothed during the Japanese tea ceremony. It's made from the tender young buds from the first harvest, which have the highest chlorophyll content and yield the most vibrant green matcha powder. Once brewed, Ceremonial-Grade Matcha has a natural sweetness and often doesn't require any added sweetener.

Culinary-Grade Matcha: Culinary-Grade Matcha is made using leaves harvested later than Ceremonial-Grade Matcha. These sturdier leaves make for a coarser matcha powder that has a more astringent flavor. Culinary-Grade Matcha—which has subcategories of its own (Classic, Kitchen, Ingredient, Café, and Premium)— is typically designed to be combined with other ingredients or used in cooking.

Mint Green Tea: Talk about a green scene! Naturally uplifting mint gets a caffeinated boost from green tea in this popular blend. Gunpowder green tea is the most popular base; it's combined with either peppermint, spearmint, or Moroccan mint to create a soothing yet energizing brew that's minty and earthy at the same time.

Sencha: Although Sencha tea is also produced in China and Korea, it is most commonly associated with Japan and accounts for over half of the country's yearly harvest. Made from small-leaf *Camellia sinensis* bushes, Sencha is a steamed green tea that has a bright flavor, ranging from vegetal to grassy, that typically isn't too bitter.

Taiping Houkui: Why is this tea from Taiping County in China's Anhui Province called "Peaceful Monkey King"? It might have

something to do with monkeys
(there are plenty of legends),
or it might have to do with the
somewhat paw-like, rolled-out
shape of the leaves. Either way,
it's a highly regarded green tea
that has a mellow flavor and a
sweet aftertaste.

Tencha: Tencha falls somewhere between traditional green tea and Matcha. It's made with the same leaves that would be used for Matcha, but before they're ground into a powder. Since the dried, crumbly leaves are quite light, you'll typically need more leaves to brew a decent cup. Tencha's flavor may vary, depending on the harvest, but tends to be mellow.

Xinyang Maojian: The tea plants used to produce this famous green tea from Henan Province in Central China are quite sturdy and thrive in the region's rocky, mountainous conditions. The common name is "Hairy Tips," referring to the small, dark green leaves covered in fine white hairs. The brewed tea is very fragrant, with a floral aroma and clean, fresh flavor.

Zhu Cha: Pow! This famous tea dates back to the Tang dynasty (about 618–907). It's commonly called "Gunpowder," perhaps owing to the leaves' rolled shapes, which resemble tiny, round pellets, or maybe due to the smoky flavor, which is rounded out with nutty and astringent undertones. Originally from China, this variety is now also produced all around the world.

Yellow Tea

Yellow tea is a rare breed. The process is similar to that of making green tea, but with an added step: The tea is sealed away and steamed to let the tea oxidize briefly before the leaves are heated. This micro-fermentation creates a chemical reaction that gives brewed tea

a mellow flavor, lacking the
grassiness and astringency of
green tea. This process also
yields a texture that's silky and
smooth-drinking.

Huo Shan Huang Ya: This yellow tea dates all the way back to the Ming dynasty (about 1368–1644). It comes from the high peaks of Mt. Huo in China's Anhui Province, and traditionally only includes cuttings with one bud and one leaf or one bud with two unopened leaves. The tea has a greenish-yellow color and a subtle, nutty flavor that may have a peppery edge.

Jun Shan Yin Zhen: This rare tea comes from Junshan Island, a tiny

island in China's Hunan Province.
The crop yield from local heir-
loom tea plants is small, and yellow tea is the most highly prized
product. The finished yellow
tea has a floral aroma; its flavor
lacks the grassiness of a green
tea and has sweet and mineral
undertones.

Kenyan Yellow Tea: Yellow tea is
rare to begin with and it's even
more rare to find it produced
outside of China. In recent years,

Kenya has dabbled in producing this time-honored tea, with fascinating results. The country's distinctive tea-growing conditions make for a brisk yet smooth yellow tea that offers a distinctly different taste experience than its Chinese counterparts.

Meng Ding Huang Ya: This yellow tea is cultivated on the foggy slopes of Meng Ding Mountain in China's Sichuan Province, where tea plants are said to have grown since the Han dynasty. The leaves are harvested in early spring; this tea has a mild but bright spring flavor, with herbal and nutty undertones.

White Tea

❧

L ess is more when it comes to white tea, which is the least-processed of all the teas.

White tea leaves are intentionally harvested before the plant's leaves fully open. These baby buds are still covered in tiny white, downy hairs, which is why it's called "white" tea. While the processing is minimal, it is exacting. Instead of being heated or processed immediately to oxidize the leaves, they're allowed to wilt and dry naturally, ideally in the sun.

The result? Some of the most delicate and freshest tea available.

While "true" white tea hails from the northern district of

Fujian, China (sort of like how Champagne is only produced in Champagne, France), similar teas are now produced all over the world. Here, we'll explore the wonderland that is white tea.

Chinese White Teas

Bai Hao Yin Zhen: The king of white teas! Also known as "Silver Needle," this is perhaps the most sought-after white tea out there. No stems or leaves are in the mix—just tender, unopened buds that resemble long, needle-like tips. This pale golden tea has a sweet, fruit-forward aroma and a light body, but with plenty of nuance; it can have fruity, floral, or herbal notes.

Fujian New Craft White Tea: This unusual white tea was developed in the late 1960s to meet growing demand for white tea. It is produced using a special process or "craft" that involves a longer-than-usual oxidation period. The result? Slightly darker leaves and a richer and more robust flavor than your average white tea.

Gong Mei: This white tea is also called "Tribute Eyebrow," based on its shape and the fact that it is said to have once been a gift to the emperor. Tribute Eyebrow tea is harvested later than White Peony and Silver Needle but has more buds than Shou Mei. Gong Mei has a rich, juicy flavor.

Nan Mei White Tea: White tea gone wild! This unmistakable white tea is made from tips harvested from wild tea plants in China's Yunnan Province. It has a vivid yellow color and a distinctive flavor that is fruity and vegetal all at once, with a touch of spice to boot. It's also one of the few white teas that is naturally caffeine-free.

Shou Mei: Also called "Longevity Eyebrow," this tea is named for its elongated and slightly bowed leaf shape, which is said to resemble the eyebrow of Shou Lao, the God of Longevity. It's made with leaves harvested later in the season than Silver Needle (see Bai Hao Yin Zhen) or White Peony. This slightly darker and bolder white tea is sometimes likened to oolong tea.

White Peony Tea: This tea contains no actual peony; some say the name refers to how the leaves delicately unfurl when steeped. Or perhaps it's the delicate, floral aroma? This tea is often considered a runner-up to Silver Needle with a stronger color and flavor and grassy undertones that call to mind a less-astringent version of green tea.

Other White Teas

Ceylon White Tea (Sri Lanka): While
Sri Lanka is most famous for its
black teas, it also produces exquisite white teas. Like its Chinese
counterparts, it is painstakingly
produced in small quantities. One
of the most popular varieties is
Ceylon Silver Tips, the country's answer to Silver Needle, a
golden-hued tea that boasts the
distinct sweetness that people
associate with Ceylon teas.

Darjeeling White Tea (India): Like other white teas, Darjeeling white teas are made from the fuzzy white buds of the tea plant. However, like other teas from Darjeeling, these white teas are singular. They have the lightness of a traditional white tea but share some of the characteristics that make its black teas famous, like a muscat-grape flavor.

Malawi Antlers White Tea (Africa): This highly distinctive white tea comes from Malawi, a country that is primarily known for black teas. Surprisingly, it's not made from buds; rather, it's made from the soft, velvety stems of the first spring shoots of the tea plant, which resemble tiny antlers once dried. The flavor is remarkably smooth and nonastringent, with floral and fruit notes.

Thai White Tea (Thailand): Although Thailand isn't the most famous tea-growing region out there, its offerings are well worth seeking out. Most tea in Thailand is produced in the mountainous northern part of the country; one of its lesser-known but worthy varieties is white tea. It has a fresh, honey-like natural sweetness that sets it apart.

Purple Tea

P urple tea isn't actually a
category of tea, like black
or green tea; rather, it refers to
teas made from rare varietals of
the *Camellia sinensis* plant with
an unusually high concentration
of anthocyanins (the same
compounds that give blueberries
their signature hue). While

purple tea leaves can follow the same processes as any other tea leaves and be made into black, green, or pu-erh teas, they're often marketed as "purple tea," based on the rarity of the plants they come from. Here are a few purple tea types to know.

Kenyan Purple Tea: Kenya's purple tea production started with a wild purple tea variety from the Assam region of India, which was used to develop a cultivar for commercial use. Typically, Kenyan purple tea is processed as a black tea. It has a flavor that is lighter than most black tea, but not as grassy as green tea.

Ye Sheng: Also referred to as "Wild Purple," this Chinese purple tea is made from the Ye Sheng varietal of *Camellia sinensis*, which grows wild in high-altitude areas in Yunnan Province. It's sometimes processed as a black tea and sometimes as a pu-erh tea; it has a complex flavor that's a little tangy and a little fruity.

Zi Juan: This tea, which is commonly known as "Purple Beauty," is made using leaves from the Zi Juan cultivar, which was developed in the late 1980s using two types of Chinese purple tea plants. The leaves from these rare tea plants can be made into high-end black, green, or pu-erh teas with a complex flavor that may have a slightly metallic astringency.

Fermented Teas

Fermented teas, also referred to as post-fermented teas or dark teas, are teas that have been exposed to microbes and allowed to ferment, sometimes for a short time and sometimes for years. (Why "post-fermented"?

Because the fermentation occurs after the oxidation step in tea processing.) In simple terms, think of foods like yogurt—this is sort of the tea version. Fermentation alters the chemistry of tea leaves, which can result in more pungent leaves but less astringency and bitterness in the finished brew. Chinese pu-erh tea is the most famous example; you'll learn more about that and more below.

Awa Bancha: This is a Japanese fermented tea that's made using late-harvested leaves. It is mainly produced on the island of Shikoku, which has a moist environment that promotes the development of the lactic bacteria that gives this tea its distinctive sour flavor. Awa Bancha's acidity is balanced by sweet notes, making for a smooth drinking experience.

Batabatacha: This Japanese fermented tea bears more than a passing resemblance to pu-erh tea and is most commonly consumed in the town of Asahi. This sweet, nutty, and smooth brew has a unique serving method: Like Matcha tea, it is frothed with a special whisk to create a soft, dense foam before you drink it.

Goishicha: Goishicha is a fermented tea from the Japanese town of Otoyo. Its production requires a two-step fermentation process that involves both mold and lactic acid; the entire process can take years. This tricked-out fermentation process gives the leaves a very pungent aroma, but it also takes away all astringency, leaving you with a sweet and sour but overall mellow tea.

Ishizuchi Kurocha: The name of this fermented Japanese tea means "Black tea of Ishizuchi," referring to the mountainous area where it's grown. During the Edo period (1603–1867), it was commonly served to pilgrims passing through on their journey to the eighty-eight temples of Shikoku, but now it's pretty rare. The tea has a low caffeine content, plenty of tannins, and a pleasant sourness.

Liu An: This fermented tea is named for the region in which it's grown in Anhui. Its processing is similar to that of Pu-erh tea. Liu An tea leaves are customarily packed in a woven bamboo basket to ferment. Flavorwise, it is earthy, may contain notes of bamboo (if packaged traditionally), and has a smooth texture with no bitterness.

Liu Bao: Liu Bao is a fermented black tea traditionally from China's Guangxi Province. It's produced much like Pu-erh teas, but it's made with medium-sized leaves and has a slightly different fermentation process. It's known for its betel (or areca) nut taste—or if that doesn't ring a bell, a flavor that's sweet and slightly fruity with a slightly woodsy bitterness.

Pu-erh Tea: Pu-erh tea, from China's Yunnan Province, is one of the most famous fermented teas out there. Made using large leaves, its production culminates in a fermentation process that may last for a few months up to a few years; like fine wines, it can become more valuable with age. This tea is often formed into cakes to ferment. The flavor is earthy, clean, and sweet.

Tengu Kurocha: This fermented tea is the result of fandom. Inspired by the nearly extinct fermented tea Ishizuchi Kurocha, a group of tea enthusiasts sought out a way to keep the tradition alive. Their answer? Tengu Kurocha, which is produced much like its inspiration in the mountainous region of Setouchi. As good as the original? You be the judge.

Tteokcha: This Korean tea—which is prepared as a round, flattened tea brick—is said to resemble a rice cake (*tteok*). After the tea leaves are picked, they are

steamed and then pounded
into shape and allowed to
ferment naturally. Once
brewed, Tteokcha often has
a deep amber color and a
fruity, earthy flavor with
hints of spice.

Tea History, Origins, Customs & Etiquette

JESSIE OLESON MOORE
ILLUSTRATED BY JESSIE FORD

PHILADELPHIA

RP Minis®
Hachette Book Group
1290 Avenue of the Americas, New York, NY 10104
www.runningpress.com
@Running_Press

Printed in China

First Edition: March 2024

Published by RP Minis, an imprint of Hachette Book Group, Inc. The RP Minis name and logo is a registered trademark of Hachette Book Group, Inc.

Running Press books may be purchased in bulk for business, educational, or promotional use. For more information, please contact your local bookseller or the Hachette Book Group Special Markets Department at Special.Markets@hbgusa.com.

The publisher is not responsible for websites (or their content) that are not owned by the publisher.

Library of Congress Control Number: 2023939504

ISBN: 978-0-7624-8515-4

HH

10 9 8 7 6 5 4 3 2 1

CONTENTS

While there is tea,
there is hope.

—ARTHUR WING PINERO

INTRODUCTION

———— ✺ ————

Tea is much more than just a beverage—it's a liquid legend that's steeped (pun intended) in history, culture, and humanity. It's a symbol of hospitality, a means of connecting with others, a source of comfort and relaxation, and part of everyday life for people all around the world. Tea has inspired countless books, poems, and works of art. It also has one heck of a backstory, complete with wars, clipper-ship races, royal drama, spy missions, and, yes, even sheep dung.

Tea is also hugely popular: It's the second-most-consumed beverage in the world after water. There are thousands of varieties in the world, a sampling of which you'll discover in this book. So how did tea go from a simple plant to a globally sipped sensation? In this book, you'll learn all about the origins and history of tea, tea customs and etiquette, and how to enjoy it in style.

The Discovery of Tea

There are a lot of stories out there about how exactly tea was discovered—most are centered around Chinese Emperor Shen Nung, circa 2737 BC.

Shen Nung was a real pre-Renaissance man and his long list of credits includes inventing the plow and introducing farming to China. He was also quite the herbalist, which is a good lead-in to the rest of the story . . .

As legend has it, Shen Nung was in his garden enjoying a nice cup of hot water. (The Chinese figured out early on that boiling water before consuming it prevented illness.) He nodded off under a large plant—a *Camellia sinensis*—and when he woke up, a few leaves had fallen in the water. Ever plant-curious, he gave the concoction a sip and found that it gave him a burst of energy. Tea was officially a thing!

Is this story, or any of its similar variations, true? Impossible to say. However,

what we *do* know is that all signs
point to China as the birthplace
and earliest adopter of tea.

Early on, tea wasn't
necessarily consumed for
pleasure. It was viewed as a
medicinal tonic and was mostly
cultivated in monastery gardens.

Eventually, that would change. By the time of the Tang dynasty (AD 618–907), new cultivation techniques had been developed and tea had been more widely adopted. The first known book about tea was published during this time—*Ch'a Ching (The Classic of Tea)* by a poet, antiquarian, and tea-obsessive named Lu Yu.

Leave-ing Home

Tea began to spread across the globe, first via Japanese monks, who brought the custom back home after studying in China.

In the twelfth century, a book titled *Kissa Yojoki (How*

to Stay Healthy Drinking Tea)
was written by a Japanese Zen
monk named Myōan Eisai;
early versions of the Japanese
tea ceremony were recorded
as early as the 1300s and this
ceremony is still a big part of
Japanese culture today.

But it wasn't until the
1600s, when traders caught
wind of the stuff, that tea's
popularity began to explode.

The Dutch really started importing tea in a big way. They established a trading post on Java, and records show that the first significant shipment of tea to Holland by way of Japan was made in 1606.

Tea began to catch on in Dutch society. From there, it spread to other Western European countries, but it was expensive, so it was mainly a drink for the rich.

England, a nation known for being tea-crazy, was actually a late adopter of the stuff.

But a royal wedding changed all that. In 1662, Charles II married Catherine de Braganza, a Portuguese princess and tea fanatic. She popularized the custom of tea-drinking in court, and you

know how people are about
the royals. Tea quickly became
de rigueur among pretty much
whoever could afford it and
became a staple in coffee
shops, which were community
hubs for conducting business.

Storms
A-Brewin'

Tea remained an upper-class beverage for a long time. Partly, this was because the British East India Company, one of the world's most powerful corporations, monopolized the tea trade and controlled the price of tea.

And then there were the taxes. During early trading years, the taxes on tea were very steep (again, pun intended)— about 25 percent.

Who likes paying taxes? Not thirsty tea drinkers!

Tea tax avoidance spawned a thriving bootleg industry. Fraudsters and smugglers

went to great lengths to avoid
taxes and maximize profits,
including mixing tea leaves
with the similar-looking leaves
from other plants, or drying
out already-used tea leaves
and combining them with iffy
ingredients, like sheep's dung,
to make them look unused
before reselling them.

While it's impossible to know
for sure, some say the illegal tea

trade may have even exceeded the legal imports during this time.

The powers that be finally took the hint that highly taxed tea was more trouble than it was worth. By the late 1700s, tea taxes were cut to a more affordable rate, and most smuggling was put to rest. But the taxes were passed on to someone else . . .

The Boston Tea Party

Hey, remember the Boston Tea Party? In case history class is a little fuzzy, here's a recap:

In May 1773, the British Parliament passed the Tea Act. This act gave the British East India Company full control over tea sales in the American colonies, with a hidden agenda of issuing heavy taxes. Within months, a protest was organized

in response—what became
known as the Boston Tea Party.

This wasn't a tea party with
scones and clotted cream,
however. It was a bunch of angry
American colonists who were
so tea'd off by this "taxation
without representation" that
they tossed 342 chests of tea
into Boston Harbor.

While the harbor probably
smelled quite cozy, this was

considered a war cry, which, in turn, rallied the patriots to come together and fight for independence.

Kind of makes today's taxes seem tame in comparison, no?

Tea Production on the Rise

———— ⚜ ————

Until the 1800s, China was the international hub of tea production. But several events would change that, including the following.

Tea Production in India

In the early 1800s, big moves
started happening to kick-start
tea production in India in order to
reduce reliance on Chinese teas.
In the early 1820s, native tea plants
were discovered in Assam, India;
production and export began not
long after this discovery.

The commencement of
Darjeeling tea production didn't
include native plants, but it

did include some spy work. Working on behalf of the British East India Company, a man named Robert Fortune went to China in hopes of stealing tea plants and cultivation secrets.

To avoid detection, he dressed up as a Chinese merchant. As far-fetched as it may seem, he had some success, and was able to bring back as many as twenty thousand tea

plants and seedlings, as well as
a handful of Chinese workers to
the Darjeeling area of India. The
combo of plants, technology,
and knowledge he brought
back played a pivotal role in
Darjeeling tea production.

The Opium Wars

Tea and war don't seem like they belong in the same sentence, but tea was actually one of the biggest culprits behind this ugly fight between Britain and China, which lasted from 1839 to 1860. The root of the war was a trade issue. The British were doing a brisk business with Chinese products, including tea; however,

the Chinese didn't want to buy
British products in return,
instead only accepting silver.

To retaliate, British
merchants started to smuggle
opium into the country, and
demanded silver for it—which
they then turned around and
used to buy tea and other items.
By the late 1830s, opium sales
were largely funding the tea trade
but had also created millions

of opium addicts in China.
Eventually, this conflict led to
war, which was a potent catalyst
for tea production in other
countries, including India and
Ceylon (now known as Sri Lanka).

Monopoly Ends

In the early 1800s, wheels were
set in motion that would eventually result in the British East India
Company losing its monopoly on

the tea trade. After that, importing tea became a free-for-all,
with enterprising importers
literally racing to get tea back to
Europe ASAP.

So began the clipper-ship
era—clipper ships have tall
masts and big sails that help
them travel at a pretty good
clip. Through the mid-1800s,
they could be seen racing
along the roundabout course

from China to the Atlantic. But
once the Suez Canal opened in
1869, steamship travel became
the dominant method of
transporting tea.

Tea Becomes an Everyday Beverage

Advancements in shipping, technology, and tea production in new areas made tea a less expensive and more widely available beverage. By the 1900s, tea had become an everyday drink for people across the globe.

But there have certainly been some fun historical sidenotes along the way. Here are just a few.

Tea-Totalers

The Prohibition era was a great time for tea. In fact, tea suddenly became the beverage of choice in all sorts of unexpected places, like clubs and hotels, as a substitute for alcohol. Of course, we now know that many of those places were, in fact, sneakily serving booze in teacups!

The Tea Bag

Did you know that the tea bag was invented in the United States? While various patents were filed roughly around the same time, one of the first that resembles what we now know as tea bags was filed in 1901, for a "tea leaf holder." The application described a "novel tea-holding pocket" constructed of open-mesh, woven fabric that kept tea leaves in place. The tea bag would continue to evolve over time, but by the 1930s, filter-paper tea bags became commonplace.

Modern-Day
Teas

These days, tea is part of everyday life around the globe and is produced on every continent except Antarctica.

There are some tea-making operations that have followed the same processing techniques for hundreds of years. Others have cropped up along the way. New cultivars are developed all the time, which only increases the number of teas to discover.

We've come a long way from tea as an upper-class-only beverage, too. While tea certainly can be part of high-class affairs, it's also a drink that is accessible to everyone.

Whether it's enjoyed loose-leaf or in bags, in black, green, or herbal form, tea is a potable phenomenon that is here to stay. Now that you understand a little more about tea's history, let's talk about different types and how to enjoy it.

Overview of Tea Grades

Tea grades aren't like school grades. Rather, the tea grading system is a means of classifying a tea based on the types of leaves contained in loose tea. A tea's grade isn't a guarantee of quality, but it does play a role.

Tea grades can be confusing. While there's a set of black tea grades that is well-recognized (see below), different countries may have their own systems. There isn't an equivalent green tea–grading system.

The most famous grade for black tea, and one you may have heard of, is OP, or Orange Pekoe. It might sound like an

orange-flavored tea, but it actually refers to a full-leaf tea without tips or buds.

Here's a rundown of some common black tea grades.

Black Tea Grades

D (Dust): This is the dust left over during the production process and is often used in tea bags.

F (Fanning): Slightly larger than dust but still small particles of tea leaves.

S (Souchong): The biggest and coarsest leaves on the plant, located near the bottom of the branch. These leaves are often used for smoked teas.

P (Pekoe): These leaves are smaller and less coarse than souchong.

OP (Orange Pekoe): The youngest and smallest tea leaves on a branch. This grade is composed of whole leaves, but no tips or buds.

BOP (Broken Orange Pekoe): OP leaves that are broken.

FOP (Flowery Orange Pekoe): Whole leaves, including tips and buds.

FBOP (Flowery Broken Orange Pekoe): BOP with some tips.

GFOP (Golden Flowery Orange Pekoe): FOP, but with tips and some golden buds.

TGFOP (Tippy Golden Flowery Orange Pekoe): Yet more golden buds than GFOP.

FTGFOP (Finest Tippy Golden Flowery Orange Pekoe): The cream of the crop, composed of golden buds, leaf buds, and young tea leaves.

Green Tea Grades

Green tea doesn't have a set of cool acronyms like black tea, but there are definitely standards. The problem? Many countries have their own systems.

Generally speaking, green teas are classified by style and quality, which has less to do with the size of the leaves and more to do with the "flush" (the harvesting period when they were picked), where they are from, how they are processed, and the flavor. While it's far from the only system, the following Japanese distinctions offer an example of how green teas may be classified, based on harvesting time.

SHINCHA

Shincha, which means "new," refers to Japanese green teas

picked during the first flush
of the season, which is typically in early April. (It's also
called *Ichibancha*, which means
"First tea.") These tender
young leaves make for teas
with a fresh scent and a sweet,

smooth, low-astringency flavor. Shincha green teas are highly prized and fetch a higher price than later-harvest teas.

NIBANCHA

Nibancha, which means "Second tea," refers to Japanese green teas from the harvest after Shincha. The leaves are typically plucked in June or July, depending on the region.

During this time, lower grades of sencha and matcha are harvested. In general, these teas will be a bit more astringent and less mellow and subtle than Shincha teas.

SANBANCHA

Sanbancha, or "Third tea," refers to Japanese green teas harvested after nibancha, typically in the late summer, from mid-August through September. Not all tea farmers choose to partake in this harvest, as the leaves are thicker and have significantly fewer nutrients than earlier harvests. Leaves taken from this harvest or later are used to make lower-grade teas, tea mixes, or bottled tea drinks.

Tea Processing

―――――― ☙ ――――――

Here's an interesting fact: All "true" teas—that is to say, tea from the *Camellia sinensis* plant, as opposed to herbal teas or tisanes—are made from the same plant. However, there are limitless

variations of tea types based on
the varietal of the plant and how
it's processed. The leaves might
be withered, dried, oxidized,
fired, and shaped—or even
ground, as in the case of matcha
green tea—to create different
tea varieties.

So, yes—as different as
black tea and green tea may
be, they're from the same
plant. It's all about how they

are processed. How does tea
go from plant to cup? Here's a
brief review.

Black Tea Processing

Let's start with black tea. There
are two key processes for
making black tea: the orthodox
process and the CTC, or crush,
tear, curl, method.

Even with the same
standard processing steps, teas

will differ, depending on the exact processing methods and where the tea is grown. So the same tea process performed in two different countries might yield a totally different product.

Orthodox Method

The orthodox method involves a four-step process of withering, rolling, oxidizing, and drying the leaves. Each step plays a crucial role in producing traditional black tea flavors.

First, the tea leaves are withered. This allows them to dry out a little, which can prevent them from flaking when they're rolled. To dry, they're laid on a mesh surface, or bamboo tray, and allowed time to rest in cool air.

Next, the leaves are rolled to encourage oxidation. They

might be rolled either by hand
or by machine. The rolling
process breaks down the leaves'
internal cell structures and
creates a chemical reaction that
helps develop flavor and aroma.

At this point, if the leaves are destined to be black tea, they go through an oxidation or fermentation process. This occurs in a warm, humid environment. During this process, enzymes and oxygen break down the chlorophyll in the leaves, giving them a darker color.

The duration of oxidation plays a big role in the finished

tea's flavor. Some teas, like oolong, are lightly oxidized and have a lighter flavor. Black teas are fully oxidized, which is what gives them their powerful flavor and reddish-brown color.

To halt oxidation, the tea leaves must be dried. This can be done in any number of ways, including pan-frying or baking.

CTC Method

The crush, tear, curl method, or
"CTC" if you're in the know, is a
process used to create shredded
tea leaves and tea pellets.

Actually, the CTC process
follows the same withering,
oxidation, and drying process
as the orthodox method. The big
difference is in the rolling stage.

During the CTC process,
leaves are rolled in machines

that have many tiny, sharp teeth. These little shark teeth—like points break the leaves into small pieces that are suitable for tea bags.

Other Tea Processing Methods

Other "true" teas generally share steps in common with black tea production, but with a few steps removed.

For instance, white teas
are the least processed—no
machinery is used, and they
simply go through the drying
process and are then
rolled by hand and dried
in natural sunlight.

Green tea doesn't go
through the oxidation
process that black
tea does, but it still
follows several of

the same steps detailed in the orthodox method. Instead of the withering step, green tea leaves are dried, either by steaming or pan-frying, so that they don't oxidize and can retain their green color. Then, they're rolled and dried again. The process might be repeated a few times before the leaves are shaped into their final form.

Pu-erh teas are unlike any other. They're post-fermented teas that are pressed into bricks and aged for several years before they are sold. The pu-erh tea oxidation occurs thanks to bacteria as opposed to enzymes in the leaves. Like fine wines, pu-erh teas are said to improve with age—some are even aged for a decade or longer!

Tea Customs Around the World

Just as there are many different types of tea, there are many different ways to enjoy it. Here are some interesting tea customs from around the world.

Britain

Is Britain's famed afternoon tea really just the result of a peckish duchess? As the story goes, around 1840, Anna Russell, Duchess of Bedford, was desperate to find a solution for the "sinking feeling" she got during the hungry hours between lunch and dinner. The solution? A light meal with tea. The custom caught on in a big

way, and it's a custom that lives
on to this day. Whether it's a
fancied-up affair with baked
goods—including scones,
clotted cream, and finger
sandwiches—or a more casual

pause in the day, what was
once a trend is still very much
part of daily life in Britain.

China

As the birthplace of tea, tea is
a hugely important and valued
part of Chinese culture. On
a day-to-day basis, tea is
simply part of life, part of
just about every meal, and it's
served everywhere. Workers

bring their own container of tea
to work.

But tea is also fancied-up
sometimes. For example,
the Chinese Wedding Tea
Ceremony, a wedding tradition
that involves the bride and
groom serving tea to their
respective families, has
been practiced for over a
thousand years. Additionally,
tea competitions are a big

deal in China—there's even a
Chinese Tea Olympics, held
in Hangzhou, featuring skill
contests for tea masters and
manufacturers.

In Tibet, the way that
they prepare it is singular:

Tibetan-style tea is made with extra-strong tea churned with yak butter and salt. This rich brew helps fortify residents and give them the calories they need to stay warm in the bitter, mountainous climate. Tibetan teahouses specialize in the stuff, which is served in small cups.

India

While tea is native to India, it wasn't commonly drunk there until production began in Assam and Darjeeling. Today, tea is consumed and sold all over India, most famously as a milky, spiced tea beverage called Masala Chai, also just called *chai*. It's sold throughout India by street vendors called *chai wallahs* ("tea people"), who serve it from big pots. Chai is also commonly served to guests upon entering the home.

Japan

The famed Japanese tea ceremony, or *chanoyu* ("hot water for tea"), is a cultural activity dedicated to the artful preparation and serving of tea. It's a ritualized practice that involves meticulously preparing the highest grade of matcha, a powdered green tea. Every aspect of its preparation, from how it is frothed, with a special bamboo whisk called a *chasen*, to the vessel used to serve it, is carefully choreographed and can take many

years to master. Typically, this
ceremony takes place in an
intimate setting with a limited
number of guests.

Turkey

Most people have heard of
Turkish coffee, but tea is just
as big a deal, if not more so, in
the country. Black tea is ubiquitous in Turkey, where it is
served in petite, tulip-shaped

glasses, almost always liber-
ally sweetened.

Turkish tea is brewed a bit
differently than your typical
black tea. It's made using a
sort of tea double boiler, with
water from the lower pot being
added to the upper pot. The
tea is strong but can be diluted
to taste with water from the
second pot.

United States

While tea at the Plaza Hotel in New York City is internationally famous, thanks to the fictional character Eloise, most day-to-day tea consumption in the United States is centered around convenience and keeping cool.

According to the Tea Association of the USA, 84 percent of the tea consumed in America is black tea, and, of that, 75–85 percent of the tea is served as iced tea. However, the COVID-19 pandemic gave boutique tea sales a big boost. Perhaps seeking out cozy comfort, Americans began buying more tea from other categories, including herbal, green, and white tea.

How to Enjoy Tea: Buying, Storing, and Preparing

———— ✼ ————

Ready to enjoy some tea? Here are some important basics you should know.

Loose Tea
Versus Tea Bags

These days, tea is pretty easy to find in both bagged and loose-leaf form. But what type should you buy?

There's nothing wrong with buying tea bags. Their convenience can't be beat, and they're available at just about every grocery store. However, tea bags may be made with lower-quality

teas and can lose their potency
faster than loose-leaf teas.

   Interested in purchasing
loose-leaf tea? Your best bet is
to purchase tea from a high-
quality purveyor with a lot of
turnover so you can be assured

that what you're buying is fresh.
If you don't happen to have a
tea apothecary nearby, there
are plenty of highly reputable
tea sellers online that sell just
about every tea you can imagine.

Tea Accessories

To make tea, you need some
basic gear. Here are some of
the essentials and some
optional accessories:

Kettle: You could boil water in a pot and pour it on top of your tea, but that can get messy (and potentially dangerous). A teakettle is really a much easier and better way to go. Both electric and stovetop varieties are available.

Teapot: While some people use the terms *kettle* and *teapot* interchangeably, they're actually different things. The teapot is the vessel to brew and serve the tea. They come in many shapes and sizes—short and stout—with a handle and a spout, including Japanese cast-iron teapots, Chinese clay teapots, tall, slim, silver teapots, and more.

Tea Cozy: A tea cozy is just as cute as it sounds. It's like a little

sweater to place over your tea-pot to keep the tea from getting cold between servings.

Tea Strainers: If you want to live *la vida* loose-leaf, you're going to need to strain your tea before you drink it. A tea strainer is like a mini-sieve that fits over your teacup to capture leaves as you pour from a teapot. A tea ball is a mesh globe that can be stuffed with loose tea before pouring water on top.

How to Store Tea

Once you've purchased tea, how can you keep it tasting its best? By sealing it off from the world. An airtight container in a cool, dark place is ideal—moisture, heat, and light can all weaken the flavor. Also, be sure to avoid storing it right next to any highly aromatic or pungent foods—your tea might absorb the flavor.

How to Brew Tea

You don't need much to make tea—just water and leaves. So, methodology matters when it comes to making the best cup. Here are a few best practices and tips.

Water

First off, since water is the vehicle for tea, make sure you use the best-quality stuff you can get your hands on. If your tap water has a good flavor, it's fine to stick with that. If you have hard water or water that has a distinctive flavor, either opt for spring water or know that the flavor of the water will impact the flavor of the tea.

For black tea, bring the water to a rolling boil and pour the hot water on the tea immediately.

For oolong tea, bring the water to a very low boil (small bubbles rising).

Green tea and white tea are often brewed with water that is just short of boiling, or water that has boiled and cooled slightly.

Prep Your Tea

Before you prepare your tea, here's something to consider:

Some people swish a little hot water in the cup and toss out the hot water before brewing tea to make sure that the tea doesn't get cold upon contact with the cup. If that sounds too fancy for you or like too much work, skip that step and move on.

If you're using a tea bag or tea bags, you can either dunk your bag in the hot water or pour water on top of it. Each method has its enthusiasts—you do you.

Using loose tea? Keep in mind that it will grow and unfurl when you put it in water, so if you're using a mesh tea ball or container, don't fill it more than halfway.

How much loose tea
should you use in a teapot?
A good general rule is one
teaspoon of loose tea leaves
per cup of water. Of course,
there are exceptions—if the
tea has really large leaves
and a teaspoon is very airy,
you might want to add a little
more tea.

Steeping Times

In terms of steeping, that depends on the type of tea and your personal preference. Many teas will include instructions, but here's a rough guide to work with:

Black teas are generally brewed for about five minutes.

Darjeeling teas typically steep slightly less time than other black teas, about three to five minutes.

Green and white teas often have briefer steeping periods than black tea, around two to three minutes. Green tea may become astringent or bitter if it is steeped too long.

Steeping time for herbal teas can vary, depending on the flavor, so you might steep your tea anywhere from a few minutes to ten minutes.

Tea
Etiquette

What are some of the dos and don'ts of enjoying tea? It depends on where you are and how you're enjoying the tea. Here are some interesting rules.

How to Hold a Teacup

In many Eastern countries, teacups have no handles. In the Western world they do, and, furthermore, etiquette dictates that the teacup should be held

by the handle. The problem?
Sometimes those tiny han-
dles are hard to hold! Don't
panic—here's how it's done.
First, place one or two fingers
of your right hand through the
hole of the handle (assuming
you're right-handed). Next,
place your thumb on top of the
handle for balance. Got any
leftover fingers? Curl them
under the handle.

Pinkies Out?

Stories abound about the origin of extending your pinky finger while drinking tea. One theory states that the custom dates back to medieval times, when people mostly ate with their hands. The pinkie was extended so it could remain clean for other activities, such as dipping into spices. No matter where the practice

came from, it's now frowned
upon by etiquette experts as an
act of pretentiousness.

To Slurp or Not to Slurp?

In the United States and
England, slurping tea is a
major breach of etiquette. Not
the case in China! Slurping
tea—loudly—is considered a
sign of respect and totally okay,

not just with tea but with any
hot liquid.

Don't Call it "High Tea"!

Americans often use the
term *high tea* to refer to a
fancy-pants tea service, but
historically speaking, there's
no high-class connection to
high tea. *High tea* referred to
the physical height of the tables
where it was served—high tops

or barlike tables. But in terms of service, high tea was served to the working classes after a shift, and typically included savory, meal-like fare. *Low tea*, on the other hand, referred to a more sophisticated sit-down tea service enjoyed at low tables loaded with finger sandwiches, scones, and clotted cream.

Milk, Not Cream

Black tea may be served with milk, sugar, or both, depending on the drinker's preference and the dominant cultural preference. But for most tea purists, adding cream to black tea is a big no-no. While whole milk's fat content helps bring out the flavor of tea, cream overpowers it, masking the flavor of tea too much to fully enjoy.

Tea-Growing Regions

For many years, tea was mainly produced in China. Now, it's grown around the globe, and different growing conditions and cultivars can yield very different products. Here are some of the largest tea-growing regions in the world.

China

China is the original tea-growing region and remains one of the world's biggest tea producers today. Tea is grown throughout the country's southern provinces, which are divided into four key regions: Jiangbei (north of the Yangtze

River), Jiangnan (south of the Yangtze River), Southern China, and Southwest China. The majority of China's tea production remains in the country. Most exports are black tea, but China also produces a variety of other teas, including green, white, yellow, oolong, and pu-erh.

India

Along with China, India is one of the biggest tea-producing countries in the world. Its three biggest growing regions are Assam, Darjeeling, and the Nilgiris. Although all these regions are in the same country, they each yield very different teas, thanks to their different elevations, climates, and plants (indigenous as opposed to imported from China). As with China, the majority of India's production remains in the country. While India is most famous for its black teas, it also produces green, white, and oolong teas.

Japan

Japan is the only big tea producer that almost exclusively works with green tea, the

majority of which is con-
sumed in-country. The major
growing regions are in the
southern part of Japan. The
two biggest production areas
are Shizuoka and Kagoshima.
Uji, in Kyoto, is also a famous
region, as it is believed to be
the first place in Japan where
tea plants were grown from
Chinese tea seeds.

Kenya

While Kenya is a fairly new tea producer, it's grown a lot in a relatively short amount of time. Tea plants were only introduced to the country in the early 1900s and production only began in the 1920s, but now it's one of the largest exporters in the world. The majority of tea in Kenya is grown in the Kenyan

Highlands, which are on either side of the Great Rift Valley, an area with tropical climates and volcanic red soil. Unlike China and India, most of Kenya's tea is exported. Kenya produces a variety of teas, including black,

green, white, oolong, and
even yellow tea.

Sri Lanka

Ceylon is the former name of
Sri Lanka, and many people
still refer to Sri Lankan tea
as Ceylon tea. Sri Lankan
tea is mainly grown in the
southern part of the country
and is often classified by the
elevation at which the plants

were grown, including low-
grown varieties, mid-grown
varieties, and—the most
highly prized—high-grown
teas. Sri Lanka is one of the
largest exporters of black
tea but the country also
produces green and white tea.